Cuba
THE LAND—THE PEOPLE

by Rick Graetz
American Geographic Publishing

The Author

President of American Geographic Publishing, Rick Graetz is a photojournalist, environmentalist, civic and political activist. He is the author of *Vietnam: Opening Doors to the World,* published by American Geographic in 1988. His private publishing imprint, Northern Rockies Publishing, has issued in recent years two editions of *Montana! A Photographic Celebration, Montana Is,* and *Montana's Bob Marshall Country.* Graetz is also part owner of and guide for High Country Adventures, a backpacking and mountaineering outfitting service. He has photographed, climbed and skied mountains and floated rivers throughout North America, South America, Hawaii and Asia.

American Geographic Publishing is a corporation for publishing illustrated geographic information and guides. It is not associated with American Geographical Society. It has no commercial or legal relationship to and should not be confused with any other company, society or group using the words geographic or geographical in its name or its publications.

ISBN 0-938314-91-2

Photographs, unless otherwise credited,
 © 1990 Rick Graetz
© 1990 American Geographic
 Publishing
P.O. Box 5630, Helena, MT 59604
 (406) 443-2842

William A. Cordingley, Chairman
Rick Graetz, President & CEO
Mark O. Thompson, Director of
 Publications
Barbara Fifer, Production Manager

Design by Linda Collins
Printed in Hong Kong

YVON CHOUINARD

Foreword

I spent approximately 25 days traveling throughout Cuba, a country about one third the size of my home state of Montana. That hardly qualifies me as an expert on this island nation. It did however, give me an opportunity to garner a good sampling of photographs of the Cuban landscape and people at work and play. And indeed, that is the purpose of this work, to present a visual impression of the people and the country. The book is not meant to imply an endorsement of a government or any political movement.

Columbus first claimed what is now Cuba for Spain in October of 1492 and Indians had settled the area well before Columbus had set foot on Cuba's north shore in Holguín Province. Since then this island has witnessed a tumultuous history, including periods of general unrest and several revolutions.

Cubans everywhere are proud of the natural wonders of their homeland. And rightly so, as Cuba is a beautiful place and many people consider it to be the most interesting of all the Caribbean islands. By far, it is the largest land mass in the Caribbean basin and therefore has more varied scenery than any other island. There are so many scenic spots that it is hard for me to suggest a favorite area.

I could spend days wandering through Old Havana. This section of the Cuban capital could be considered one of the world's treasures. Many of the buildings, some dating back to the 1500s, are well preserved. Cuba's oldest town, Baracoa, established in 1512, was of immense interest, and I only regret that I didn't have more time to spend there. The mountainous country from Santiago de Cuba eastward toward Baracoa represents a region I would like to explore further.

My favorite drive was on the road that follows the seashore at the foot of the lofty Sierra Maestra to the west of Santiago de Cuba to Pilón. The mountain relief here is impressive, as some of the peaks rise abruptly to 6,000 feet and higher. Couple this with the aqua-shaded Caribbean waters sending huge waves crashing onto the rocks and cliffs, and the viewing is magnificent.

The colonial sector of Trinidad, Cuba's second-oldest city was a wonder, featuring the oldest buildings in the country. The cobblestone streets, narrow alleys and old buildings made this place a worthwhile visit. Many people consider Cienfuegos to be Cuba's most beautiful city. I won't quite make that claim but I thoroughly enjoyed this south-central Caribbean

Above: The royal palm, the Cuban national tree.
La palma real, el árbol nacional de Cuba.
Left: A reef near Cayo Largo.
Un arrecife cerca de Cayo Largo.

Facing page, left to right:
Rick Graetz.
El autor, Rick Graetz.
On the streets of Cárdenas.
En las calles de Cárdenas.
A resident of Trinidad.
Una residente de Trinidad.

Front cover: From El Morro toward the Havana skyline. YVON CHOUINARD
Vista de La Habana desde el Morro.
Back cover, top left: Yvon Chouinard fishing near Cayo Largo, photographed by a local fisherman.
Yvon Chouinard pescando cerca de Cayo Largo. La fotografía fue tomada por un pescador local.
Right: Young athletes running the steps of Cross Hill at Holguín.
Un grupo de atletas jóvenes sube corriendo una escalinata en Holguín. YVON CHOUINARD
Bottom: The Valle Palace in Cienfuegos is now a first-class restaurant.
El Palacio Valle en Cienfuegos ahora es un restaurante de primera clase.
YVON CHOUINARD

3

coastal city. The Valle Palace, Cienfuegos Bay, and the city square were just a few places I found appealing in Cienfuegos.

And then there was Cayo Largo, a beautiful key off the southern coast toward Jamaica. Most of the keys in the area are uninhabited and reefs jutting from the turquoise Caribbean waters provide outstanding snorkeling. The isolated white sand beaches bordered by tropical vegetation paint an idyllic setting. And there were many other areas of Cuba, such as Camagüey, Holguín, Manzanillo and Bayamo that I would have liked to see more of.

The one regret I have is that my grasp of Spanish is limited and therefore I didn't have the opportunity to talk to more of the people in the many cities and towns I traveled through. There is far more to a nation than scenery. Getting to know the people is a prerequisite to a great journey, and I hope to know Cuba and its people better in the future.

———————————

There are many people to thank for all the help I was given to make this project successful. Ariel Ricardo in Washington, DC, believed in my idea for a book and secured permission for me to travel to Cuba. In Miami, Sylvia Vieta and Rafael Licea, Executive Director of the Kiwanis Club of Little Havana, and Waldo Castro-Molleda of the Latin Chambers of Commerce and Industry gave me valuable insight into what to see in Cuba. And Manny Perez-Hernandez of Perez-Hernandez Promotions & Advertising Group in West New York, New Jersey, provided important guidance.

I'd also like to thank Leon Perez, Hermis Campos and Fina de la Rosa León for their help as well as our drivers in Cuba, Adealle, Domingo, Alfonso and Herman.

Nikon FM cameras were used to photograph Cuba and I thank Nikon for providing some of the extra equipment I needed.

Most of all I would like to thank my wife Susie, and Yvon Chouinard for accompanying me on the longest of my three trips. They both helped me with photography I needed for other purposes as well as for additions to this work.

Rick Graetz

Above: *The birthplace of José Martí. El lugar de nacimiento de José Martí en La Habana.*
Top: *Statue of José Martí in Cienfuegos. Estatua de José Martí en Cienfuegos.*

There have been many heroes in Cuba's history, but the most revered is the poet and writer José Martí. Born in Havana in 1853, Martí was a driving force behind the Cuban independence movement in the late 1800s. He lived abroad for many years in exile and helped raise funds and garner resistance to events in Cuba. Eventually he returned to Cuba to begin the nation's second war for independence. Three months later, on May 19, 1895, he was killed in combat in Dos Ríos near Santiago de Cuba.

Facts on Cuba

The "Pearl of the Caribbean," as some people call Cuba, is located just to the south of the Tropic of Cancer. Serving as a gateway to the Caribbean and the Gulf of Mexico, it is situated approximately 90 miles south of the Florida Keys, 130 miles east of Mexico's Yucatán Peninsula, 87 miles north of Jamaica and 48 miles west of Haiti.

Cuba is made up of more than 3,700 islands, keys and islets, taking up a total area of 42,615 square miles, with the main island of Cuba consisting of 40,508 square miles. The main island has about 3,560 miles of of shoreline and is known for its beautiful mixture of white sandy beaches, cliffs, coral reefs, mangrove swamps and bays.

Seventy-five percent of the main island surface is made up of relatively flat plains, with the balance in three distinct separate mountainous areas. The predominant mountain areas are in the southeast of Cuba and consist of the Sierra Maestra, the Sierra de Nipe, Sierra de Nicaro, Sierra del Cristál and Cuchillas de Toa. The country's highest peak, Pico Turquino, rises to 6,177 feet in the Sierra Maestra to the east of Santiago de Cuba. The Sierra de Escambray, located in the southern midsection of the island around Cienfuegos and Sancti Spíritus provinces, is the second-highest range in the country. This highlands area is broken up into two separate ranges, the Sierra de Trinidad and the Sierra de Sancti Spíritus. Pico San Juan at approximately 3,800 feet is the highest point. The third grouping of mountains, located in Pinar del Río province in the western part of Cuba, is known as the Cordillera de Guaniguanico. It consists of the Sierra de los Organos and the Sierra del Rosario. The highest point in this area is Pan de Guajibón Mountain at 2,283 feet.

The nation's longest river, the Río Cauto, is 229 miles long and drains the Sierra Maestra area.

Cuba's climate is tropical. It has a mean annual temperature of about 77 degrees Fahrenheit. The coldest month, January, averages about 72 degrees and August, the hottest, 84 degrees. The rainy season extends from May to October and, during the period of June through November, the island can experience hurricanes. The eastern part of the country, around Guantánamo Province in southeastern Cuba, is the driest but the mountains just above this area receive the most precipitation.

More than 10 million people call Cuba home. With almost 2 million people, Havana—La Habana in Cuba—is the largest city, followed by Santiago de Cuba. The people speak Spanish and, for the most part, there are no local dialects.

The main crops for export are sugar, citrus fruits, tobacco and coffee. The monetary system is based on the peso, which is composed of 100 centavos.

—*Rick Graetz*

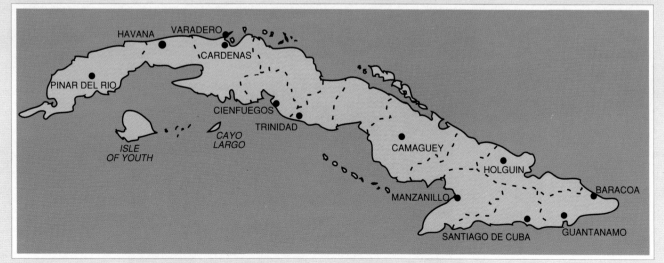

Right: *La Fuerza Castle in Old Havana*
El Castillo de la Fuerza, en La Habana Vieja.
Below: *From the Malecón (seawall) toward El Morro Castle in Havana. Vista del Morro desde el Malecón en La Habana.*
Bottom: *The cannon-shot ceremony at the La Cabaña Fortress, Havana. Every night at 9 p.m. the cannon is fired to commemorate a tradition of announcing the city gates' closing. El Cañonazo de las 9. Cada noche a las 9 p.m. se dispara un cañonazo desde la fortaleza de La Cabaña para conmemorar la tradición de anunciar el cierre de las puertas de la ciudad.*

Facing page: *Havana, looking south from the Havana Hilton. La Habana, mirando al sur desde el Habana Hilton.*

Above: *Fishing for blue marlin off Havana.*
Pescando cerca de La Habana.
Right: *Havana, looking west from the Riviera Hotel.*
La Habana, mirando al oeste desde el Hotel Riviera.

Left: *Playing ball in Havana near the university.*
Jugando en La Habana cerca de la universidad.
Above: *Sunset from Havana's Malecón.*
Puesta del sol desde el Malecón en La Habana.

Facing page: *The Cathedral of Havana, completed in 1776, in Old Havana.*
La Catedral de La Habana, terminada en 1776, en La Habana Vieja.

Left: *Young track athletes in Havana.*
Dos pequeños corredores en La Habana.
Above: *Havana, looking northwest from the Habana Hilton.*
La Habana, mirando al noroeste del hotel Habana Hilton.

Facing page: *An example of a mansion formerly belonging to a wealthy Cuban. Many such houses now are used for diplomats and for government purposes.*
Mansión en que vivió antiguamente una familia cubana adinerada. Muchas mansiones de este tipo se utilizan ahora como residencías de diplomáticos u oficinas gubernamentales.

Overleaf: *From the Malecón looking southwest at Havana.*
Desde el Malecón mirando al sudoeste.

Above: In Cathedral Square of Havana is El Patio Restaurant, the former mansion of the Marquis de Aguas Claras.
El restaurante El Patio, antiguamente la mansión del Marqués de Aguas Claras, en la Plaza de la Catedral de La Habana.
Right: Looking north from above the University of Havana steps.
Mirando hacia el norte desde la escalinata de la Universidad de La Habana.

Facing page: The former Cuban capitol, now headquarters for the Academy of Science.
El antiguo capitolio, ahora la Academia de Ciencias.

Above: *A Havana mansion.*
Una mansión de La Habana.
Right: *A street in Old Havana.*
Calle en La Habana Vieja.

Far right: *Havana as seen south of*
the Habana Hilton.
Vista de La Habana, mirando hacia
el sur desde el Habana Hilton.

Above: *The show at the nightclub Tropicana. In 1989, this nightclub— with its internationally famous show—was celebrating its 50th anniversary.*
El espectáculo en el cabaret Tropi- cana. En 1989, este centro nocturno, con espectáculos de fama inter- nacional, celebró su L aniversario.

Facing page: *The Havana skyline. La Habana.*

Above: *Along the Malecón in Havana.*
A lo largo del Malecón en La Habana.
Left: *From El Morro Castle looking toward the Havana skyline.*
Vista de La Habana desde el Castillo del Morro.

Facing page: *The view of Havana west from the Habana Hilton.*
Vista de La Habana, mirando hacia el oeste desde el hotel Habana Hilton.

Above: *Cigar factory in Manzanillo.*
Una tabaquería en Manzanillo.
Right: *The Grand Theater of*
Havana.
El Gran Teatro de La Habana.

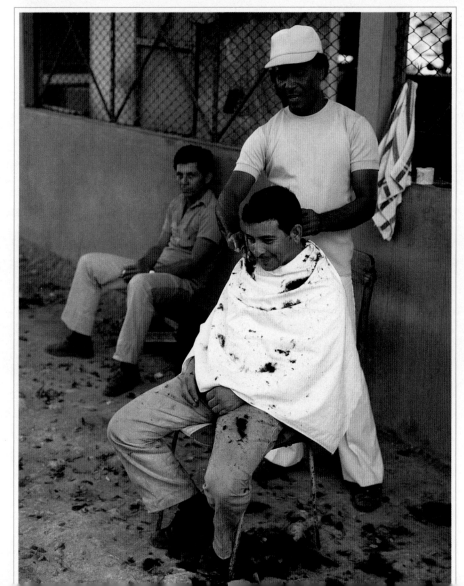

Left: *Barber in Pilón.*
Barbero en Pilón.
Above: *The steps at the University of Havana.*
La escalinata de la Universidad de Habana.

Facing page: *On Obispo Street in Old Havana. The building on the left is the oldest in the city, built about 1552. The taller, pink building is the Ambos Mundos Hotel. The top floor windows, surrounded by white, open from the room where Ernest Hemingway worked on* For Whom the Bell Tolls.
La calle Obispo en La Habana Vieja. El edificio a la izquierda, construído alrededor de 1552, es el más antiguo de la ciudad. El edificio rosado es el Hotel Ambos Mundos. Las ventanas pintadas de blanco en el piso superior corresponden a la habitación donde Ernest Hemingway escribió el libro Por Quién Doblan las Campanas.

Overleaf: *Viñales Valley in Pinar del Río Province.*
El Valle de Viñales en la provincia Pinar del Río.

Above: *Harvesting rice in Pinar del Río Province.*
Cosechando arroz en la Provincia de Pinar del Río.
Right: *El Castillo de las Nubes.*

Facing page: *In the Sierra de Los Órganos near the town of Viñales.*
En la Sierra de Los Órganos cerca del pueblo de Viñales.

Above: *Sierra del Rosario in Pinar del Río Province.*
La Sierra del Rosario en la Provincia de Pinar del Río.
Right: *A happy greeting in Perché.*
Un saludo alegre en Perché.

YVON CHOUINARD

Viñales Valley in Pinar del Río Province.
El Valle de Viñales en la Provincia de Pinar del Río.

Above: *A sugar plantation in Pinar del Río Province.*
Un campo de caña de azúcar en la Provincia de Pinar del Rio.
Left: *Harvesting sugar cane near Manzanillo.*
Cortando caña de azúcar cerca de Manzanillo.

Facing page: *In the Sierra de los Órganos east of La Palma.*
En la Sierra de los Órganos al este de La Palma.

Above: *La Bayamita in the Sierra Maestra Mountains—a doctor's office on the lower level, with his residence on the upper floor.*
La Bayamita en las montañas de la Sierra Maestra. En el primer piso de la casa se encuentra el consultorio de un doctor, que reside en el piso superior.

Left: *Soroa resort area in the Sierra del Rosario Mountains.*
Soroa en las montañas de la Sierra del Rosario.

Above: *A rural school in the Sierra Maestra near Pilón.*
Una escuela rural en la Sierra Maestra cerca de Pilón.

Right: *Sierra del Rosario.*

Facing page: *In the Sierra de los Órganos.*
En la Sierra de los Órganos.

Above: *A farm in the Sierra de los Órganos.*
Una granja en la Sierra de Los Órganos.
Right: *Near the town of Pinar del Río.*
Cerca de la ciudad de Pinar del Río.

Children at La Esperanza.
Niños en La Esperanza.

Left: *Sierra del Rosario Mountains.*
Above: *Grinding coffee beans in Pinar del Río Province.*
Moliendo granos de café en la Provincia Pinar del Río.

Above: *Cayo Largo in the Caribbean.*
Cayo Largo en el Caribe.
Left: *Internacional Hotel on Varadero Beach, built in the 1950s.*
El Hotel Internacional en Varadero, construido alrededor de 1950.

Facing page: *La Esperanza.*

Overleaf: *Cayo Largo, one of the many keys off the south Caribbean coast of Cuba.*
Cayo Largo, una de las numerosas isletas de la costa sur de Cuba en el Caribe.

Above and facing page: Cayo Largo.
Right: Bougainvillea. Buganvilla.

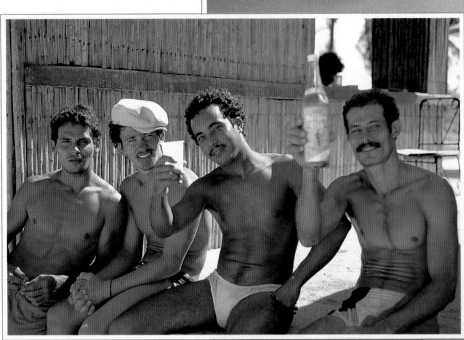

Above: *Partying at Coral Beach.*
Festejando en Playa Coral.
Right: *Aerial view of Varadero on Cuba's Atlantic shore.*
Vista aérea de Varadero en la costa atlántica de Cuba.

Overleaf: *Cuba's north shore from Varadero.*
La costa norte de Cuba desde Varadero.

Above: *Along the Caribbean coast below the Sierra Maestra.*
En la costa sur, al pie de la Sierra Maestra.

Left: *Running from falling rock on the road that runs from west of Santiago de Cuba along the Sierra Maestra.*
Un campesino y su asno esquivan un desprendimiento de rocas sobre una carretera, que parte del oeste de Santiago de Cuba y corre a lo largo de la Sierra Maestra.
Facing page: *The Sierra Maestra.*
La Sierra Maestra.

Above: *The former Dupont mansion Xanadu at Varadero. With a nine-hole golf course, the estate once served as a winter hideaway for Irenee Dupont.*
Xanadú, la antigua mansión de la familia Dupont en Varadero. La residencia, con su campo de golf de nueve hoyos, era la casa de invierno para Irenee Dupont.
Right: *East of Santa Cruz.*
Al este de Santa Cruz.

Above: *Ernest Hemingway's house, now the Hemingway Museum, in San Francisco de Paula. This was the author's home from 1939 until shortly before his death in 1961.*
El Museo Hemingway en San Francisco de Paula. Ernest Hemingway vivió en esta residencia, Finca La Vigía, desde 1939 hasta poco antes de su muerte en 1961.
Left: *An old fort in Cojimar, the town from which Hemingway fished and which he used as his setting for* The Old Man and the Sea.
Una vieja fortaleza en Cojimar, el pueblo desde donde Hemingway salía a pescar y que utilizó para su obra El Viejo y el Mar.

Above: *The Gaviota Hotel on
Varadero Beach.*
El Hotel La Gaviota en Varadero.
Right: *Varadero beach scene.*
En la playa de Varadero.

Above: Los Cactus Hotel at
Varadero Beach.
El Hotel Los Cactus en Varadero.
Right: Cayo Blanco.

Clockwise from above: A 1940s model car.
1950 Mercury near Santa Maria.
1928 Ford in Rafael Freyre, Holguín Province.
Buick, circa 1953, in Havana.

Un auto de los años 40 **(arriba)**, un Mercury de 1950 cerca de Santa María **(a la derecha)**, un Ford de 1928 en Rafael Freyre, en la Provincia de Holguín **(abajo, a la izquierda)**, y un Buick de 1953 en La Habana.

Above: *Dusk comes to Baracoa in eastern Cuba. Established in 1512, Baracoa is the oldest community in the nation.*
El crepúsculo cae sobre Baracoa, en el extremo oriental de Cuba. Baracoa, la ciudad más antigua del país, fue fundada en 1512.
Right: *Sunday washday near Cajobabo in eastern Cuba.*
Dos campesinos friegan su camión el domingo cerca de Cajobabo, en la zona oriental de Cuba.

Facing page: *Imías on the Caribbean coast of eastern Cuba.*
Imías, en la costa sur de la zona oriental del país.

Overleaf: *The Sierra de Nicaro near Cajobabo.*
La Sierra de Nicaro cerca de Cajobabo.

YVON CHOUINARD

Above: *Fishing along the Caribbean coast near San Antonio del Sur.*
Pescando a lo largo de la costa caribeña al este de Cuba cerca de San Antonio del Sur.
Left: *Along Baracoa's Malecón as evening falls.*
El Malecón de Baracoa, al atardecer.

Above: *An oasis in a dry area near San Antonio del Sur.*
Un oasis en medio de un zona árida cerca de San Antonio del Sur.
Right: *Washday near Cajobabo.*
Una campesina lava la ropa en un río cerca de Cajobabo.
Facing page: *Flora of the dry coastal area east of Guantánamo.*
Flora de la árida zona costera al este de Guantánamo.

YVON CHOUINARD

Above: *A resident of Santiago de Cuba.*
Un residente de Santiago de Cuba.
Right: *Along Cuba's south Caribbean coast below the Sierra Maestra in the El Papayo area.*
Area de El Papayo, en la costa del Caribe al pie de la Sierra Maestra.

Above: *At Veguita del Sur in the Sierra de Nicaro.*
En Veguita del Sur en la Sierra de Nicaro.
Right: *The Sierra de Nicaro near Macambo. This is perhaps Cuba's driest area and in many places resembles the northern Sonoran desert.*
La Sierra de Nicaro cerca de Macambo. Esta es quizás la zona más árida de Cuba, y en muchos lugares se parece al desierto de Sonora.

Above: *Throwing a fishing line along the Caribbean coast of eastern Cuba near San Antonio del Sur.*
Lanzando un anzuelo en la costa de San Antonio del Sur.
Facing page: *Fishing boats in Cienfuegos Harbor.*
Barcos de pesca en la Bahía de Cienfuegos.

Above: The Valle Palace in the
Punta Gorda district of Cienfuegos.
El Palacio Valle en el Distrito de
Punta Gorda en Cienfuegos.
Right: Fishing in Cienguegos Bay.
Pescando en la Bahía de Cienfuegos.

Facing page: A Sunday afternoon
jam session in Cárdenas.
Una sesión de música en la tarde de
un domingo en Cárdenas.

YVON CHOUINARD

Above: *Perché, a fishing village, jutting out into Cienfuegos Bay.*
Perché, un pueblo de pescadores, se adentra en las aguas de la Bahía de Cienfuegos.
Left: *Bougainvillea.*
Buganvilla.

Facing page: *Early morning light over Cienfuegos Harbor.*
La luz matutina sobre el puerto de Cienfuegos.

Above: *A wooden carving at Guamá.*
Una escultura de madera en Guamá.

Right: *At Guamá, a reconstructed Taíno Indian village on Treasure Lake. The area was named for an Indian chief who fought the Spanish invaders. Life-sized carvings of the Indians showing them going about their daily lives are scattered throughout the island.*
En Guamá, un pueblo reconstruido de los indios Taínos en la Laguna del Tesoro, hay estatuas de tamaño real de los indios en sus actividades diarias por toda la isla. El área fue bautizada con el nombre de un jefe indio que luchó contra los conquistadores españoles.

Above: *Camagüey.*
Right: *A tinajón in Camagüey. Originally used for collecting rain water, the size and quantity of these wide-mouth jars were signs of a family's wealth.*
Un tinajón en Camagüey, originalmente utilizado para recoger agua de lluvia. El tamaño y la cantidad de estos jarrones de boca ancha en una casa indicaban la posición social de la familia.

Facing page: *Children in Holguín.*
Niños en Holguín.

Above: *Transportation in Pilón.*
El transporte en Pilón.
Left: *Treasure Lake in the Guamá area.*
Laguna del Tesoro en Guamá.
Overleaf: *Varadero from the air.*
Vista aérea de Varadero.

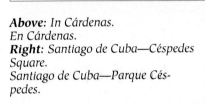

Above: *In Cárdenas.*
En Cárdenas.
Right: *Santiago de Cuba—Céspedes
Square.*
*Santiago de Cuba—Parque Cés-
pedes.*

Facing page: *Children in Cárdenas.*
Niños en Cárdenas.

Above: *A resident of Cárdenas in front of an old church and a statue of Christopher Columbus.*
Un residente de Cárdenas, en frente de una iglesia y una estatua de Cristobal Colón.
Right: *Horses and buggies are a popular means of transportation in Cárdenas, the picturesque city on Cuba's north coast.*
Las calesas tiradas por caballos constituyen un popular medio de transporte en Cárdenas, una pintoresca ciudad de la costa norte de Cuba.
Far right: *From Puerto Boniato looking toward the Big Stone (Gran Piedra) near Santiago de Cuba.*
Vista de la Gran Piedra, cerca de Santiago de Cuba, desde Puerto Boniato.

Above and left: *Santiago de Cuba.*

Facing page: *The harbor at Santiago de Cuba.*
El puerto de Santiago de Cuba.

Left: *The bay at Santiago de Cuba from Morro Castle.*
La Bahía de Santiago de Cuba desde el Castillo del Morro.
Above: *Two residents of Trinidad.*
Dos residentes de Trinidad.

Above: *Countryside between Guantánamo and Santiago de Cuba. El paisaje campestre entre Guantánamo y Santiago de Cuba.*
Left: *Céspedes Square in Santiago de Cuba, Cuba's second-largest city. Parque Céspedes en Santiago de Cuba, la segunda ciudad más grande de la isla.*

Facing page: *Sierra Maestra from Morro Castle, Santiago de Cuba. La Sierra Maestra desde el Castillo del Morro, Santiago de Cuba.*

Above: *Santiago from Puerto Boniato.*
Santiago desde Puerto Boniato.
Right: *Playing basketball in the harbor area of Santiago de Cuba.*
Un partido de baloncesto en el área del puerto en Santiago de Cuba.

Facing page, top: *The cathedral in Santiago de Cuba, built in 1523.*
La Catedral de Santiago de Cuba, construida en 1523.
Bottom: *From the Gran Piedra, looking west toward Santiago de Cuba. This big rock sits at an altitude of 3,300 feet above sea level. Desde la Gran Piedra, mirando al oeste hacia Santiago de Cuba. Esta roca gigantesca se encuentra a una altitud de 3,300 pies sobre el nivel del mar.*

Above: *From the San Luís Valley, the Sierra de Trinidad, part of the Sierra de Escambray east of Trinidad.*
La Sierra de Trinidad, que forma parte de la Sierra del Escambray al este de Trinidad, vista desde el Valle de San Luís.
Left: *A street scene in colonial Trinidad.*
Escena de una calle en la Trinidad colonial.

Facing page: *A Trinidad girl celebrates her 15th birthday, marking an event very special in the life of each Cuban girl.*
Una joven de Trinidad celebra sus 15 años, una fiesta tradicional en Cuba.

Above: *The Santísima Trinidad
Church in colonial Trinidad.
La Iglesia de la Santísima Trinidad
en la cuidad colonial de Trinidad.*
Right: *Children in Trinidad.
Niños en Trinidad.*

Facing page: *The Brunet Palace in
Trinidad's Main Square.
El Palacio Brunet en la plaza
principal de Trinidad.*

Above: In Santiago de Cuba, Céspedes Square looking at the oldest house in Cuba, on the left. It belonged to Diego Velázquez and was built between 1516 and 1530. The main structure on the right is the provincial administration building.

En Santiago de Cuba, el Parque Céspedes mira hacia la casa más antigua de Cuba (a la izquierda). Pertenecía a Diego Velázquez y fue construida entre 1516 y 1530. El edificio principal a la derecha es la sede de las oficinas de la administración de la provincia.

Right: On a side street of colonial Trinidad.

En una calle de Trinidad colonial.

The main square in Trinidad, Cuba's second-oldest city, established in 1514. This square today looks much as it did in the early 1800s.
La plaza principal en Trinidad, la segunda ciudad antigua en Cuba, establecida en 1514. La plaza principal parece igual como en su era en los 1800s.

Above: Cuba's north shore from
Varadero.
*La costa norte de Cuba desde
Varadero.*
Top: Musicians in colonial Trinidad.
Músicos en la Trinidad colonial.
Right: In Trinidad.
En Trinidad.

Above: *Pico Turquino from 6,177 feet. This mountain in the Sierra Maestra, with an elevation of 6,542 feet, is Cuba's highest.*
Vista del Pico Turquino desde una altura de 6,177 pies. Situado en la Sierra Maestra y con una altura de 6,542 pies, es la más alta elevación de Cuba.
Right: *Trinidad wedding.*
Boda en Trinidad.